# H. H. RICHARDSON

# H. H. RICHARDSON

## Three Architectural Tours

### Ken Bresler

To Marly & Eliza

# Table of
# Contents

# H. H. Richardson: A Life, Briefly

**Henry Hobson Richardson** was the leading American architect of the nineteenth century. He is the only American architect after whom a style is named. The Richardsonian style dominated the United States for the last two decades of the nineteenth century, even after Richardson's early death.

Richardson was born on September 29, 1838 to wealthy parents on Priestley Plantation in St. James Parish, Louisiana, and grew up largely in New Orleans. He was admitted to West Point, but because he stuttered, his parents encouraged him to pursue a civilian career. Richardson wound up at Harvard University, where he made valuable contacts that later advanced his career.

Richardson graduated from Harvard in 1859, and traveled to Paris. In 1860, he entered l'Ecole des Beaux Arts to study architecture. When the Civil War interrupted his family's financial support, he started working as a draftsman for French architects.

After the war, Richardson returned to America. He began as an architect in New York and quickly made his mark. He even-

H. H. Richardson in Henry Adams's study, photograph by Marian Hooper Adams, 1884. Collection of the Massachusetts Historical Society.

tually designed buildings there and in Boston, Chicago, Pittsburgh, Cincinnati, Washington, D.C., and elsewhere. He contributed to the completion of the New York State Capitol in Albany.

H. H. Richardson is best known for designing Trinity Church in Copley Square. That commission also led to his return to the Boston area. To supervise Trinity Church's construction, Richardson moved his home and studio, from Staten Island and Manhattan respectively, to Brookline. Then he joined Boston society.

Richardson was an architect for only 18 years, but he achieved much in his short life. He influenced numerous architects, including Frank Lloyd Wright, Charles McKim, and Stanford White. His influence survived him. For example, chapter 2 includes two buildings, one completed in 1995, the other in 2011, that pay tribute to him. Chapter 3 includes two buildings that were built in his style by his successor firm after he died on April 27, 1886. He was 47.

Here are three tours of Richardson's work in the Boston area. The first tour is of Copley Square, where Richardson designed four buildings: his masterwork, Trinity Church, the Trinity Church Rectory, the Brattle Square Church, and a brick residence. As a matter of fact, if you stand at one intersection and turn 180 degrees, you can see the first three buildings.

The second tour is of Harvard University, Richardson's alma mater, and Harvard Square. The tour starts at Richardson's Sever Hall in Harvard Yard, proceeds to Richardson's Austin Hall in the North Yard, where the law school is located, continues to two recent Harvard Law School buildings that echo Austin Hall, and ends at a country-style wooden residence near Harvard Square.

The third tour is not a walking tour of buildings, but rather a rolling tour on what is now the Green Line of the Massachusetts Bay Transportation Authority, including photographs and former sites of demolished train stations that Richardson designed for a bygone era.

**H. H. Richardson: Three Architectural Tours**

Richardson designed two buildings within Boston's boundaries that are not on the first tour. They appear in the appendix.

Richardson's legacy survives, even if many of his buildings have not. He changed the way that America looks.

# Copley Square

## WALKING TOUR

*Before you take this tour: The interiors of two buildings on this tour are open to the public and well worth seeing. If you want to go inside Trinity Church, check trinitychurchboston.org for its visiting hours. If you want to go inside the Brattle Square Church/First Baptist Church, call 617-267-3148 to find out when it will be open or to make an appointment. You don't need binoculars or field glasses, but consider taking them to view the frieze, the carved decorative band, high on the First Baptist Church's tower.*

**Of the 45 surviving buildings** that H. H. Richardson designed, four are in the Copley Square area. With almost a tenth of Richardson's extant work on display, Copley Square is a permanent blockbuster exhibition. The four Richardson buildings that you're about to view will be roughly in the order in which he designed them, so you will be able to see him mature as an architect.

*Start in Copley Square. Walk to 164 Marlborough Street. Start on Dartmouth Street facing Trinity Church with your back to the Boston Public Library. Go left on Dartmouth Street. When you reach Commonwealth Avenue and before you cross, look to the right.*

From the side of Commonwealth Avenue where you are standing, you can see the tower of Richardson's Brattle Square Church rising above Back Bay. At the top of the tower, on the corners, look for sculpted angels blowing long horns. The church is the second site on the walking tour.

*Cross Commonwealth Avenue and continue on Dartmouth Street. When you get to Marlborough Street, turn left. Stop in front of the corner house, 164 Marlborough Street.*

# Benjamin W. Crowninshield House
### 164 Marlborough Street, southwest corner of
### Dartmouth and Marlborough Streets

This house, built in 1870, represents H. H. Richardson's early work. It is only his fourth known building and is not recognizably Richardsonian. As for being Romanesque, a style that Richardson adopted and advanced, the building displays only one small Romanesque detail, repeated twice and practically hidden.

The house is four stories tall, with the top floor behind a mansard roof. (A mansard roof has two slopes; the lower slope approaches vertical, the upper one approaches horizontal.) The facade is basically flat, except for a boxy entry bay.

Richardson later became a master of massing—the arrangement of a building's elements, how it sits. But the massing of the Crowninshield House is, frankly, mundane.

In later buildings, Richardson *incorporated* details. In the Crowninshield House, he *attached* details here and there. Between the second and third floors, a line of blue-and-white glazed ceramic tiles alternates with green-and-white tiles. The tiles are square and stand on their points. The design of repeating squares occurs under the eaves between the brackets.

On each of the two corners of the entry bay, at the second floor, is a twisted column of bricks, called a Salomonic or Solomonic column. To accent this touch, some bricks are black; they were blackened with pitch or dipped in tar. The black probably dates back to Richardson's design; a Richardson building completed a year after the Crowninshield House used blackened bricks. Other details in the brick, such as the stringcourses (the recessed lines running around the basement), are also blackened.

The lintels (the stones above the window openings) are carved sparsely with plant and flower motifs. On the entry bay, in an opening in the brick parapet above the second story, is a floral design in metal. A canopy of wrought iron and glass over the door adds interest. Carved in stone over the door is a monogram, BWC, for the original owner, Benjamin W. Crowninshield.

Crowninshield and Richardson probably knew each other at Harvard. Crowninshield graduated in 1858, a year before Richardson. The house was used as a college dormitory beginning in the early 1960s. Until 2017, Bay State College leased and used it as a dorm, which explains the prominent fire escape that mars the house's facade. As of this writing, it is vacant.

A plaque to the right of the door notes that the house is on the National Register of Historic Places. (The other three Richardson buildings on this walking tour are also on the register). As of this writing, you can peek through the glass of the front door and see imposingly tall ceilings. Richardson's heavy wood staircase, now painted white, rises to the fourth floor, but the metal railing at the bottom is almost certainly not original. Neither is the front door. Under the sidelights next to the front door are ceramic squares.

One Richardson scholar had unkind comments about the house. Henry-Russell Hitchcock's criticism included this: "The windows are tall, narrow and curiously spaced. The pair on the right side of the house breaks the symmetry quite arbitrarily...."

However, you can view the asymmetry as whimsical. Richardson used both symmetry and asymmetry masterfully.

Donlyn Lyndon, an architecture writer, had this to say: "This early work shows signs of repressed talent."

*Cross Marlborough Street and walk away from Dartmouth Street. View the side of the house over the low brick building that is attached to the right.*

The side of Crowninshield House ends after the first window bay. The two drainpipes are the dividing line between Richardson's work and the building next to it.

The window bay is two stories high, with a surprisingly blank wall above it. The tile decoration carries around the corner from the front for two tiles, one tile on each side of the bay.

*Cross Marlborough Street and turn right on Dartmouth Street. View the house from the side.*

On the side of the entry bay, the twisted-brick column is topped with a Romanesque capital. This is the hidden Romanesque detail. It is a hint of Richardson's future reliance on the Romanesque style. (More on the Romanesque style soon.) The column on the other side of the entry bay has a matching capital.

On the side chimney is a medallion framed by brick. The actual painting on the medallion is recent, although it is unclear whether the design dates back to Richardson's time.

Combined with the left side of the chimney is a bay window. You'll see this combination—chimney and bay window—again soon. The lintels are carved with a saw-toothed design.

To the left of the Crowninshield House is a building with two entrances, 312 and 314 Dartmouth Street. Although the building, with its mansard roof, tiles, and carved lintels, resembles the Crowninshield House, no evidence exists that H. H. Richardson designed it. A vertical line running through the bricks indicates that the Crowninshield House is a separate building from 312 and 314 Dartmouth Street. And some of the latter's features, such as the doorways, are distinctly un-Richardsonian.

*Continue on Dartmouth Street to Commonwealth Avenue. Turn left on Commonwealth Avenue, and walk down the Mall (the center of the boulevard). Stop before you reach Clarendon Street. Stand opposite the huge circular window on the church.*

**H. H. Richardson:** Three Architectural Tours

# Brattle Square Church

**110 Commonweatlh Avenue,
southwest corner of
Commonwealth Avenue
and Clarendon Street**

This stretch of Commonwealth Avenue is defined by the undulating fronts of row houses, in red brick, brownstone, and marble tones, with bay windows and elegant staircases stretching down to the sidewalk. Suddenly, a massive flat wall of buff Roxbury puddingstone presents itself to the street. The trim is sandstone.

This church is particularly important because it was H. H. Richardson's first major commission and the first building in which he used Romanesque forms extensively. A major supporter of the new church construction was Benjamin Crowninshield's father, so Richardson's work on the Crowninshield House may have led to this commission.

*American Architect and Building News,* March 24, 1894, reproduced in Jeffrey Karl Ochsner's *H. H. Richardson: Complete Architectural Works.* In the foreground on the right is Richardson's Trinity Church Rectory. (See page 27.)

Romanesque is a pre-Gothic style of architecture from Europe, particularly France and Spain. Richardson didn't so much revive Romanesque as adapt it, borrowing from other styles and ages, including Syrian Christian architecture, and fashioning an American style called Richardsonian Romanesque, or simply Richardsonian.

Although most churches are laid out in the shape of a cross, this one is in the shape of a T. The reason is the snug plot that Richardson was given to work with. You are looking at the end of the crossbar of the T, called the transept. The vertical part of the T (called the nave), where most of the seating is arranged on either side of a long aisle, extends to the left, parallel with Commonwealth Avenue.

The large circular window, called a rose window, is an eight-petaled flower in typical Romanesque form. The church has three rose windows. Each stained-glass petal is separate. Richardson designed similar windows for later buildings.

The flower is framed by two circles of stone whose colors change subtly and randomly from stone to stone. Richardson used this polychromatic stone device elsewhere on the church and in later buildings. Above the circular window are two vertical rectangular windows. On top of these windows is an unusual window; you can view it as two intersecting valentines, one inverted, or as two ovals crisscrossing each other. Richardson used this figure in other works too.

Under the rose window are seven windows whose lintels are saw-toothed. Richardson used saw-toothed lintels on the Crowninshield House, which you just saw, and the Hayden Building. (See page 89.)

Not all of the Commonwealth Avenue side of the church is Richardson's work. The portion to the right of the door, marked "110" (for 110 Commonwealth Avenue), was added later.

Richardson designed the church for a Unitarian congregation whose previous home was in Brattle Square in Boston. It was built between 1870 and 1872. Four years after the church was completed, the Uni-

**H. H. Richardson: Three Architectural Tours**

tarians went broke paying for it. The congregation dissolved and the building was empty for several years. The Baptists bought it in the early 1880s. In descriptions of Richardson's work, this church is sometimes called the Brattle Square Church, even though it is not in Brattle Square, and sometimes the First Baptist Church, even though Richardson did not design it for Baptists.

The church has a third name, a nickname. Because of the trumpeting angels on the four corners of the tower, some people have called it the Church of the Holy Bean Blowers.

---

*Cross Clarendon Street, but stay on the Commonwealth Avenue Mall. Kitty-corner from the church, face the tower.*

---

You are looking at the church's most beloved feature, its tower. The tower is the only component that Richardson later liked. The tower resembles an Italianate campanile, a free-standing bell tower.

When the church was vacant in the nineteenth century, people discussed the possibility of tearing it down—but leaving the tower to preside over a small park. Citizens may even have raised money or pledges for the project.

The tower is 176 feet high. It starts, from the top down, with a red-tiled pyramidal roof, which is not visible from this angle. Immediately under the roof on all four sides is a series of seven corbeled arches. The corbels, the stone supports projecting from the wall, are a common Richardsonian touch.

Next comes the frieze, the carved decorative band. It is by Frédéric Auguste Bartholdi, who also designed the Statue of Liberty. It depicts four of the sacraments: baptism (facing Clarendon Street), communion (facing Commonwealth Avenue), marriage (facing Newbury Street), and death (facing Dartmouth Street). The faces are reportedly those of prominent residents of Greater Boston, such as Henry Wadsworth Longfellow, Ralph Waldo Emerson, and Nathaniel Hawthorne. The frieze was not carved in a studio, but in place, by artisans on scaffolding.

Separating the sacraments at each corner are the trumpeting angels. They were originally gilded, but their current stone color makes it appear as if the angels have stepped out of the frieze.

If you don't have binoculars or field glasses, you can view close-up photographs of the frieze, as of this writing, on the church's website, firstbaptistchurchofboston.com, and on Wikipedia under "First Baptist Church (Boston, Massachusetts)."

Under the frieze on each of the tower's four sides is a large arch, into which two smaller arches are nestled. The large arches are framed on top with polychromatic stone and are sliced horizontally with louvers. Pigeons fly in and out of the tower here.

A particularly graceful detail is on the corner of the tower facing you: a sheaf of five columns. One column plunges below the rest toward the ground, although it's not always visible under the ivy.

Under each large arch is a sequence of five narrow arched windows with polychromatic stone over them. Under this sequence on the Commonwealth Avenue side of the tower, another sequence of narrow arched windows—three ascending windows—hints at steps. Depending on the season, these windows may be covered by ivy. The windows line up vertically underneath the first, third, and fifth of the five windows above them.

The tower stands on four piers, which create a porte-cochère, a carriageway.

---

*Cross Commonwealth Avenue. Stand on Clarendon Street across from the church.*

---

This is the church's main entrance. The three arches and Romanesque carvings are characteristic of many of Richardson's buildings.

You are looking down the length of the church, at the bottom end of the T. The gable is filled with another rose window. This one is divided into quadrants by a cross made of columns. The columns are noteworthy for two reasons. It is jarring to see horizontal columns. The word "column" implies verticality (as in "column of numbers").

**H. H. Richardson: Three Architectural Tours**

And classical architecture prescribes the elements of a column's base and capital (the top)—and the base and capital differ from each other. Here, the elements are mixed, resulting in columns whose bases and capitals are combined, columns that are symmetrical at either end.

The height of the gable gives you an idea of the height of the church's lofty interior. The main worship space is in the shape of a T, but the building itself is not. The right corner of the building is taken up by the tower. The left corner is filled with a chapel, which was originally used for the Sunday school.

*Cross Clarendon Street to the church.*

The portico floor is tiled. The doors, three in front of you and a fourth to the left, are made from diagonal boards and have massive, crescent, medieval-looking hinges.

The interior is a soaring but simple space, which as of this writing, needs millions of dollars in repairs. Some of Richardson's stenciling design has been painted over. The Baptists added the balconies after they bought the church; they are not Richardson's design. They also added a stained glass window by Louis Tiffany to the left of the altar.

*Walk on Clarendon Street away from Commonwealth Avenue. Turn right on Newbury Street. Walk past one building. Turn right and look through the alley at the church.*

You are looking at the end of the transept, the crossbar of the church's T shape. (You saw the other end of the transept on the Commonwealth Avenue side). Above the rose window are two rectangular windows. Above them are seven small circular windows. Below the rose window are seven vertical windows that match the Commonwealth Avenue facade. (You can see only six from here.)

*Return to the corner of Newbury and Clarendon Streets. Face Clarendon Street. The brick building across Clarendon Street is the next stop on the walking tour.*

The Trinity Church Rectory before an extra floor was inserted—and before the lot across the street was built on, or at least fully built on. One doesn't always pay attention to basement windows, but these windows, aligned with the windows above, add to the building's gracefulness. So does the curved window under the stairs. Because of cars parked on both sides of the street in the twenty-first century, you generally can't see the basement windows from across Clarendon Street. The photograph was taken between 1879, when the rectory was completed, and 1893, when the extra floor was added. Photograph courtesy of Historic New England.

# Trinity Church Rectory
### 223 Clarendon Street,
### northeast corner of Clarendon and Newbury Streets

So far the walking tour has covered Richardson's works in the chronological order of their construction. This building is slightly out of order. It is the Trinity Church Rectory, the residence for the church's rector. It was built in 1879, or two years after Trinity Church, the next and last site on the walking tour, was dedicated.

The facade features a Syrian arch over a recessed entry. The arch is so much a signature of Richardson's work that it is sometimes called a Richardsonian arch. The arch is off-center. Above the door is a small eight-petaled flower of polychromatic stone, which Richardson used elsewhere in his work and which brings to mind the rose windows in the Brattle Square Church. To the left of the door in the recessed entry is a set of wonderfully arranged windows. The door itself is constructed of diagonal boards, a common Richardson touch that you saw at the Brattle Square Church.

The flowers and foliage in the second-story panels were created by carving the bricks. It is the finest example of Queen Anne Revival brickwork in Back Bay, wrote Margaret Henderson Floyd, a Richardson scholar.

The original resident of the rectory was Phillips Brooks, a friend of H. H. Richardson. Brooks, a bachelor, was succeeded by a rector with a family, whose members needed a larger home. In 1893, after Richardson had died, the three-story building was expanded to the current four stories. The third story you see now was inserted into the building. The second and third stories are identical, except for the carved brick panels decorating the second story. The consensus is that inserting an extra story did not really harm the building's aesthetics, but you are looking at a building that is higher and less compact than Richardson intended.

The fourth floor of the Clarendon Street facade has a gable on each side. The windows within the gables are not symmetrical. One set of windows is set into an arch. The other set is a pair of side-by-side rectangular windows. The gables have in-laid brickwork called marquetry. Above the rectangular windows is an arch design in the bricks.

The two dormers between the gables are not symmetrical; the right dormer is much narrower than the left. The placement of the windows on the whole facade is "rhythmic," as architecture writers Susan and Michael Southworth put it.

**H. H. Richardson: Three Architectural Tours**

*Cross Newbury Street and stand on the corner of Newbury and Clarendon Streets, kitty-corner from the rectory. Turn toward the rectory again.*

The rectory's endpiece on Newbury Street is symmetrical. Richardson merged the chimney into the window bay. (He did something similar on the Crowninshield House.) The window bay ends above the second floor. When the extra floor was added to the rectory, the window bay was lowered from two-and-a-half stories to two. Compare it now with the photograph on page 27.

*Turn around and continue on Clarendon Street. Stop when you get to Boylston Street.*

Across Boylston Street, on the corner of Boylston and Clarendon Streets, is Trinity Church. Before viewing it fully, turn around again and look at the Trinity Church Rectory and the tower of the Brattle Square Church. The intersection of Boylston and Clarendon Streets is the only place in the world where it has ever been and is possible to view three Richardson buildings from the same spot, simply by turning 180 degrees.

*Cross Boylston Street. Take a half-right turn and walk on a diagonal, with the church on your left.*

## Trinity Church

You are walking along what used to be Huntington Avenue. Before this part of it was closed off, Huntington Avenue ran through Copley Square's plaza. Closing off the street made the plaza more inviting, but harder to comprehend the ingeniousness of Richardson's plan for a trapezoidal site.

*Stop when you get to the statue of Phillips Brooks, and face it.*

To the left is the parish house, where the church's offices have been located. It is linked to the church, but separated from it by a cloister, a covered passageway. The cloister is formed by alternating columns (which are round) and piers (which are octagonal). The colonnade of columns and piers effortlessly becomes an open-air stairway as it merges with the parish house. Donlyn Lyndon called it "surely one of the smoothest, most carefree gestures in American architecture." The stairs lead to a chapel.

This is a beautiful spot. While you're here, step back to the walkway, lean your head back, and gaze up at the church and its towers. The view gives you a sense of this building's power.

---

*Continue walking counterclockwise around the church to its front, the facade facing the plaza. Step back at least to the unpaved area.*

---

You are looking at H. H. Richardson's most celebrated work and a masterpiece of American architecture. Trinity Church consistently places high in polls among architects. In 1885, architects named it the best building in America; in 1956, the fourth best; in 1985, the sixth best. In 1980, the U.S. Postal Service featured Trinity Church on a stamp. Only 15 other American buildings appeared in the series.

Brattle Square Church was nearing completion when the competition to design Trinity Church began. The recognition that Richardson received from his earlier design, particularly the tower, led to his invitation to join the competition. In the plans that he submitted for Trinity Church, he drew the Brattle Square Church's tower in the background.

Several members of the Trinity Church building committee were Richardson's classmates at Harvard. When his design was accepted, Richardson was only 34 years old, and only five years into his career as an architect. His design not only cemented his professional reputation, but changed his life as well. In spring 1874, right before construction began, Richardson moved his home and studio from New York City to Brookline.

What you see, however, is not Richardson's winning design. Richardson grew as an architect as construction progressed between 1872 and 1877, and so did his architectural vision. Richardson once said about the drawings that he submitted to the competition, "I really don't see why the Trinity people liked them, or, if they liked them, why they let me do what I afterwards did."

Even after the church was dedicated in 1877, Richardson was not finished. The facade that you are looking at was then flat, and the two towers in front were simpler. Richardson didn't like the effect, drafted some changes, and urged the church to rebuild. Unfortunately, Richardson didn't live to see the changes.

Between 1894 and 1897, after Richardson had died, his successor firm, Shepley, Rutan & Coolidge, built the front towers and the portico with the three deeply recessed arches. The portico is based on the Romanesque church of St. Trôphime in Arles, in the south of France. The firm's design is possibly more elaborate than what Richardson had envisioned.

The demands of a compact plot precluded a typical crucifix design with a long nave (the main aisle and seating section). Instead, the church is laid out like a Greek cross, almost the shape of a plus sign. While most churches' towers are in front (imagine a traditional New England church with a white spire) or off to the side (recall the Brattle Square Church), Trinity's main tower is centered. Richardson wrote that a church and its spire often compete for precedence, but that here he created a tower as the central mass and grouped the nave and transept, which crosses the nave, around it.

Richardson's design for Trinity's main tower may have been inspired by the Cathedral of Salamanca in Spain. Richardson's tower has four sides, which lead to an eight-sided roof. The roof has red tile, as do many of Richardson's buildings.

---

*Go inside the church. As you enter, notice the doors made from diagonal boards, with massive, medieval-looking strap hinges.*

---

Merely entering the church can be a religious experience, as writer Susan Wilson noted. "The interior of the church is one of the most serene architectural spaces in the world," wrote James F. O'Gorman, a

Richardson scholar. The ceiling in the tower soars 103 feet above you; the ceilings in the barrel vaults, 63 feet. The paintings and stained glass are by noted artists.

*After viewing the interior, return to the front. Go out the church's doors, but don't step down from the portico yet. Turn left and walk down the length of the portico. When you get to the stairs, stop and look at yourself reflected across the street in the building.*

The building you're looking at was called the John Hancock Tower when it was completed in 1976 for the John Hancock Life Insurance Company. It's now called 200 Clarendon Street (even though 120 St. James Street is one of the building's addresses; you can see the address across the street). This mirrored skyscraper, across St. James Street from the church, was conceived as an "invisible building." One reason for the mirrored design was to avoid crowding and detracting from Trinity, reflecting it instead of overpowering it.

Nonetheless, the building did harm the church, if not aesthetically, then structurally. Trinity Church is built on landfill (which is why the neighborhood around Copley Square is called Back Bay), and is supported by four huge granite pyramids and 4,500 wooden piles. Construction of 200 Clarendon Street caused the local water table to drop, which in turn caused Trinity Church to twist and crack. The church sued the John Hancock Company, which settled the suit in 1987 for several million dollars..

*Turn left and continue walking counterclockwise around the church.*

The central tower is nearly identical on all four sides. One of the challenges of this plot was to design a church that is conspicuous from all sides. Richardson succeeded magnificently.

*Continue walking on Clarendon Street behind Trinity Church.*

The curved back of the church is called the apse. The altar is located inside. To the right of the apse are stairs. Go up the stairs to see the lovely garden, called a garth, between the church and parish house. You may have already seen it from another angle.

To the left of the garth is a cloister leading to a door. On a cloister wall near the door is a tablet placed by Boston architects, calling Trinity Church the "noblest work" by Richardson.

As you walk behind the church, you can see the tower of the Brattle Square Church on Clarendon Street.

*Walk around to the front of the church once more. Go to the last site on the walking tour, the Boston Public Library, which faces Trinity Church from across Dartmouth Street.*

*Stand on the Dartmouth Street stairs. With your back to the library, stand about 10 feet to the left of the statue on the left.*

Between Trinity Church and 200 Clarendon is the mirrored skyscraper's predecessor, the first John Hancock Tower, built for the insurance company in 1947.

The John Hancock Tower appears to pay tribute to Trinity Church. Both buildings have pyramidal roofs and stubby wings.

You are looking at an architectural triptych: Trinity Church, which dominates and possesses Copley Square; the earlier John Hancock Tower, which evokes Trinity Church; and the mirrored 200 Clarendon Street, which reflects it.

Throughout his lifetime, Richardson suffered from many illnesses, but finally succumbed to kidney failure. The architect's friends used to say, "Richardson would never take time to die." But when he did, he died busy and he died young.

On the day he died, Richardson told his doctor that he wished "to live two years to see the Pittsburgh Court-house and the Chicago store complete," referring to the Marshall Field Wholesale Store. He wanted to be judged and remembered for those works in progress. "If they honor me for the pigmy things I have already done, what will they say when they see Pittsburgh finished?" he wondered.

What did they say? The Allegheny County Courthouse in Pittsburgh is still acclaimed. The Marshall Field Wholesale Store, demolished in 1930, is still influential. (See pages 90-91.) But Richardson is judged and remembered largely for Trinity Church.

Henry Hobson Richardson died on April 27, 1886. He was 47 years old. His funeral was held in Trinity Church; Phillips Brooks conducted the service.

Brooks's spoken eulogy probably resembled his essay that was published half a year later. Brooks wrote about Richardson: "All his buildings took possession of the earth they stood on, as he himself, without pretentious self-assertion, took possession of every scene in the midst of which he stood."

Henry Hobson Richardson was an architect for only 18 years. But his influence endures.

**H. H. Richardson: Three Architectural Tours**

# Harvard Square

## WALKING TOUR

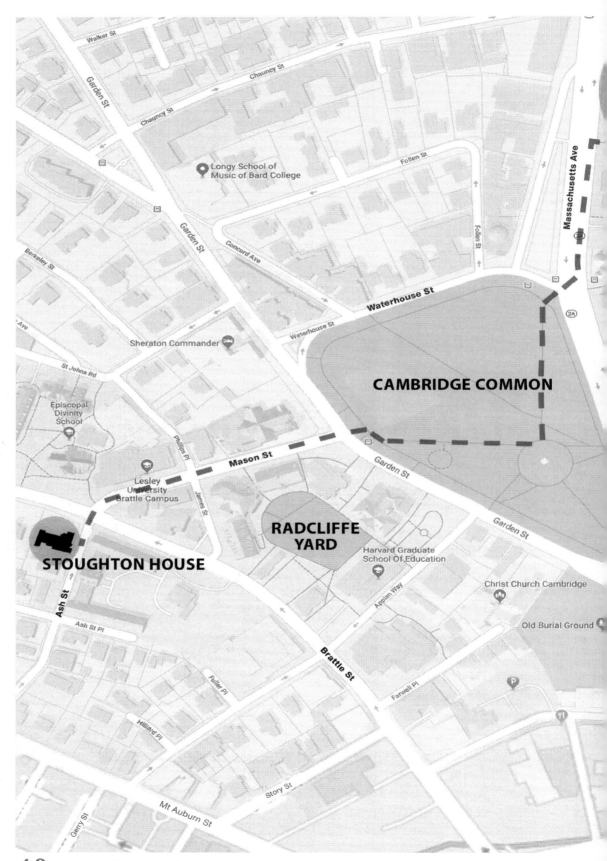

H. H. Richardson: Three Architectural Tours

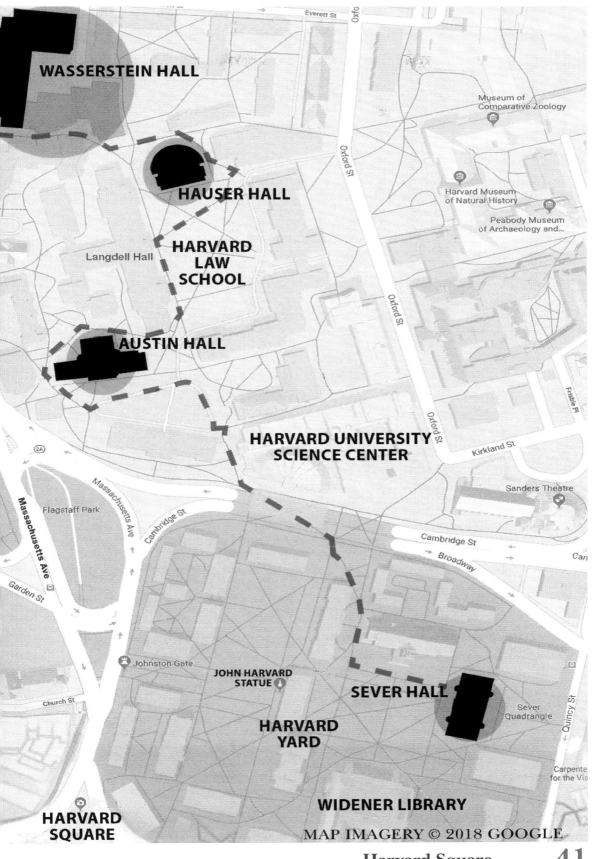

WASSERSTEIN HALL

HAUSER HALL

HARVARD
LAW
SCHOOL

Langdell Hall

AUSTIN HALL

Museum of
Comparative Zoology

Harvard Museum
of Natural History

Peabody Museum
of Archaeology and...

Oxford St

HARVARD UNIVERSITY
SCIENCE CENTER

Kirkland St

Frisbie Pl

Sanders Theatre

Flagstaff Park

Massachusetts Ave

Cambridge St

Cambridge St

Broadway

Can

Massachusetts Ave

Garden St

Johnston Gate

JOHN HARVARD
STATUE

SEVER HALL

Sever
Quadrangle

Quincy St

Church St

HARVARD
YARD

Carpente
for the Vis

WIDENER LIBRARY

HARVARD
SQUARE

MAP IMAGERY © 2018 GOOGLE

*Go to Harvard Square. Use the map on pages 40 and 41 to find Sever Hall.*

**You are about to see three buildings** by H. H. Richardson and two that pay tribute to his style. For a biography of Richardson, a son of Harvard, see page 9.

# Sever Hall

"This is without question one of Richardson's greatest works of architecture. It is, moreover, an almost unique masterpiece of the incredibly difficult art of building in harmony with fine work of the past and yet creating a new style for a new day."

– Henry-Russell Hitchcock,
*The Architecture of H. H. Richardson and His Times*

*Face the main facade of Sever Hall, the one looking on the rest of Harvard Yard, not the one looking on Quincy Street.*

Sever Hall (pronounced to rhyme with "fever") is serene and dignified. The most immediately noticeable feature is the Syrian arch, leading to a deep entrance. The arch is so much a signature Richardson feature that it is also called a Richardsonian arch.

Sever Hall's brick construction comports with and honors its fellow buildings in Harvard Yard, most of which are brick. It nods a tribute to classical architecture. Above the arch is a slightly projecting bay, topped with a triangular pediment, an element found in Greek and Roman temples, and other classical and classically-influenced structures.

The three-and-a-half story building is symmetrical and largely horizontal. The horizontal character is broken up by two turrets. Carved brick panels of foliage appear on the facade. The hipped roof (it slopes on all four sides) is red tile, which Richardson used for many of his buildings. The trim is Longmeadow sandstone.

Richardson won the commission for Sever Hall in 1878, nineteen years after he graduated from Harvard in 1859. Anne E. P. Sever bequeathed the money for the building in memory of her late husband, James Warren Sever, an 1817 Harvard graduate. The building was completed in 1880.

Sever Hall announces its year of completion three times. The date "1880" appears below the pediment on the facade facing the rest of Harvard Yard. The right chimney on this side has the year in Roman numerals, MDCCCLXXX, carved into its bricks. Carved into the left chimney is "Anno•Domi," short for "Anno Domini," the unabbreviated version of "A.D." On the opposite facade, the one facing Quincy Street, "MDCCCLXXX" is also carved into the right chimney, with "Anno•Domi" carved into the left.

*Walk to the arch.*

**H. H. Richardson: Three Architectural Tours**

The arch has acoustic properties that give it the name "The Whispering Arch." If you station a companion at one end of the arch, go to the other end, face the bricks, and speak or whisper, your companion will be able to hear you.

The arch is elaborate and deep enough to have a small indented space with room for a small person to step into. If you're small, step in; if you're not, lean in. Then whisper a message to your companion on the other side.

Lovers love Sever Hall and use the whispering arch for romantic messages. The acoustic properties are probably unintentional.

The boards making up the door are diagonal, a common Richardson touch, as are the massive strap hinges.

Sever Hall contains classrooms and offices. It is open to people associated with Harvard University, but not the public. People teach, learn, and work in the building, and in the past, tourists and other visitors have disrupted those endeavors. Please obey the "No Trespassing" sign.

*Go counterclockwise around the building.*

The Quincy Street facade has another pediment, smaller than the one on the front. Above it, a broad bay swells slightly. This facade has two turrets, as on the main facade. A line of attic windows breaks the roof.

Notice two minor details that will become important later during this tour: the window heads and the brick frames around the windows. The window heads are the elongated sandstone trapezoids capping the mullions. (The mullions, in turn, are the vertical dividers, made of brick, between the windows.) The bricks framing the windows do not come to a 90-degree angle. Rather, the bricks are curved. The curved bricks make the mullions look almost like slender columns.

You'll see these window heads and mullions again soon.

Continue counterclockwise around the building. The north facade has the Harvard seal carved into its bricks: a shield, three books, and the university motto "Veritas." The first two books are open; the third is face down. The first book represents the Old Testament, the second, the New Testament, and the third, a testament to be written at the Second Coming of Jesus Christ. In 1643, the official seal depicted the third book face down, as if it has not yet been revealed, but later official versions depict it face up. Here is one of the occasional appearances at Harvard of the original version of its seal.

Like many of Richardson's buildings, Sever Hall is eclectic. Architectural historians have noted, in addition to the Syrian arch and classically-inspired pediments, Colonial, Georgian, and Queen Anne Revival influences. The massive hinges on the main facade's doors are medieval-looking.

Richardson's biographer, Mariana Griswold Van Rensselaer, called Sever Hall "an epitome of architectural excellence" and "among the most perfect creations of modern architecture."

"I love Sever Hall," architect Robert Venturi has said. "I could stand and look at it all day."

*Use the map on pages 40 and 41 to walk to Austin Hall.*

# Austin Hall

Henry-Russell Hitchcock, a Richardson scholar, considered Austin Hall "one of Richardson's greatest works."

The building is mostly symmetrical. The major exception is the off-center turret, which leads to what was once the dean's office on the second floor. The turret resembles the four turrets on Sever Hall.

Austin Hall is shaped like a T. You are looking at the crossbar of the T. The rest of the T extends behind the building. The central part of the building in front of you consists of two stories. Each wing is one story and contains a large amphitheater-like lecture room. The rest of the T behind the building contains a third lecture room.

A mock courtroom takes up most of the second floor of the central part of the building. The space was once the law school library.

The entablature is carved with a quotation from Exodus 18:20: "And Thou shalt teach them ordinances and laws and shalt shew them wherein the way they must walk and the work they must do."

The portico has three Romanesque arches, as do many of Richardson's buildings. The arches meet at two places, and above where they meet are eight-petaled rosettes in polychromatic stone, another common Richardson feature. The belt course between the first and second floors is a mosaic checkerboard design. You will see both the eight-petaled rosettes and the stone checkboard again soon.

Austin Hall is named in memory of Samuel Austin, who was born into a commercial family. The money for the building was donated by his brother Edward Austin, who did not attend Harvard and detested lawyers.

Austin Hall opened its doors to students on September 27, 1883. It was completed in 1884, but 1883 is the date that appears on two chimneys. After it opened, Austin Hall *was* Harvard Law School. Now it is one of the law school's several buildings.

*Walk closer to the building.*

Demarcating the two wings of the building from the central part are drainpipes. Each drainpipe is anchored to the building by a carved-stone grotesque, a serpent-like creature coiled around the drainpipe.

Two other mystical creatures are nestled into the space where the left side of the turret meets the facade.

To the left of the portico is a pilaster, a flattened column, surmounted with an angelic face. At the bottom of the pilaster is a fierce mythical animal. Under the animal is a rectangular panel with H. H. Richardson's monogram. Look closely and you can discern "HHR," interwoven with what look like drafting tools. This may be the only example

**H. H. Richardson:** Three Architectural Tours

of Richardson's having "signed" a building. The panel includes a Romanesque knot-like design.

*Step into the portico.*

"The intricate Romanesque detailing of the porch is one of his most memorable sculptural creations," wrote Richardson scholar Margaret Henderson Floyd. Generations of law students have been amused by the faces carved in yellow Ohio sandstone. The work is by John Evans, a carver who worked on several Richardson buildings. The detailing may have been damaged decades ago by cleaning.

On the portico is a door to the turret. As is typical for Richardson's doors, it is made of diagonal boards.

Austin Hall contains classrooms and offices. Like Sever Hall, it is open to people associated with Harvard University, but not the public. Please obey the "No Trespassing" sign.

*Leave the portico and walk clockwise around the building to the side.*

Here is another of the occasional depictions of Harvard's seal with the third book face down. It is unclear why both of Richardson's buildings at Harvard are carved with its original seal.

*Continue to the back of Austin Hall.*

Opinions are divided on the rear of the building. Van Rensselaer exulted that "no piece of work that Richardson ever executed exceeds the back of this building for purely architectural beauty—for the virtues of good proportion, harmonious outlines, well-arranged features, artistic treatment of surfaces, and simple dignity of expression." Hitchcock, however, called it "matter-of-fact."

The chimney at the second-floor level is decorated with a six-pointed star. It resembles a Star of David, but has no known connection to Judaism.

On the left, neither the glass canopy nor the staircase that it covers is original.

In the rear, the tan-painted doors with diagonal planks may be original, but the paint is almost certainly not. The doors were probably originally dark-stained wood.

---

*Continue walking to the fourth side of the building.*

---

This side, too, has a Harvard seal. From here, you can see eight-petaled rosettes on the second story that also appear on the main facade.

The windows are deeply set (giving the building a sense of strength and solidity) and the mullions (the vertical dividers between the glass panes) are stone. You will see these details again soon.

This is the only academic building that Richardson designed in stone. He designed the rest, such as Sever Hall, in brick. However, all of Richardson's public libraries (in Malden, Quincy, Woburn, and North Easton, all in Massachusetts) are stone. Austin Hall, of course, contained the law school's library, and its building material and design have much in common with Richardson's libraries.

---

*Use the map on pages 40 and 41 to walk to Hauser Hall.*

---

**H. H. Richardson: Three Architectural Tours**

# Hauser Hall

As you approach Hauser Hall, a Harvard Law School building completed in 1995, the first thing you are likely to notice is the Richardsonian arch, just as you probably first noticed Sever Hall's arch. Hauser Hall, a neo-Richardsonian building, pays tribute to both Sever and Austin Halls.

The arch is set into stark and stunning white granite. It is carved in a white-and-white checkerboard design, echoing Austin Hall's polychromatic checkerboard stonework.

*Walk around the building counterclockwise.*

On the back of Hauser Hall, look at the window heads: The stone trapezoids resemble those of Sever Hall. The brickwork around the windows on Hauser Hall looks like the slender, semi-detached, column-like brickwork on Sever Hall.

Hauser Hall was designed by KMW Architecture. Bruce A. Wood, the *W* in the firm's name, told the author that the firm paid homage to Austin Hall and Sever of its own volition, not at the law school's direction. He is proud that the quality of the stonework on Hauser Hall at least matches that of Austin Hall.

*Use the map on pages 40 and 41 to walk to Wasserstein Hall.*

# Wasserstein Hall

Like Hauser Hall, Wasserstein Hall has a Richardsonian arch in white stone (several arches, actually), and pays homage to Austin Hall. Completed in 2011, it was intended to unify Harvard Law School's diverse architectural styles. It was designed by Robert A. M. Stern Architects in cream-colored Indiana limestone.

The south entrance, named Kumble Courtyard, has five arches. On the courtyard's exterior, two arches faces south, and one faces Massachusetts Avenue. (These are the three arches visible in the photograph.) Inside the courtyard are two more arches. One houses an entryway that leads into the building's interior. The fifth arch is nearly "blind"; that is, it is not open. A window is set into it.

The north entrance, at the opposite end on Massachusetts Avenue, has three arches: two open arches and one built into the wall, into which an entryway is set.

The arches are an obvious Richardsonian touch, but there are more touches. The architects designed Wasserstein Hall's deeply set windows and stone mullions to recall Austin Hall.

*Use the map on pages 40 and 41 to walk to the Stoughton House.*

**H. H. Richardson:** Three Architectural Tours

Circa 1883. The recessed loggia is open, as Richardson designed it. Photograph courtesy of Historic New England.

# Mrs. M. F. Stoughton House
## 90 Brattle Street,
### west corner of Brattle and Ash Streets

You have seen Richardson's work in brick and stone. Now you see it in wood. All three of his buildings in Cambridge are turreted.

The house is basically horizontal, like Sever Hall. A Richardson scholar, James O'Gorman, called the Stoughton House "a wooden variation of the disciplined form of Sever Hall."

The Stoughton House, like many of Richardson's buildings, is eclectic. It is considered to be in the Shingle style, whose structures have flat shingled surfaces, an exterior horizontality, and an interior horizontal flow. The house is L-shaped, which is typical of Shingle-style houses. The Norman turret (recalling the architecture of Normandy) is at the reentrant angle (the crook of the L), where Richardson often placed turrets.

It was completed in 1883 for Mary Fisk Stoughton, a widow. The house was originally built with a porch on the first floor and a recessed loggia on the second floor, a feature that Richardson used in other houses, both city and country. It may have been an echo of houses in Richardson's native Louisiana. The house also shows the influence of the Colonial style.

The house was altered soon after it was completed. Mrs. Stoughton was dissatisfied with it, but the exact nature of her dissatisfaction is unknown. The loggia was enclosed with windows. Later owners hired Richardson's successor architectural firm to extend the rear of the house. Thus, the Ash Street facade is wider than Richardson designed. The door knocker on the Ash Street side is not original.

It is hard to view the Stoughton House because of the brick wall that blocks much of it. View the house from three places: from across Brattle Street, on the sidewalk where the driveway meets the walk, and on Ash Street. A color photograph from 1997 appears on the back cover of this book.

This is a private home. Please do not enter the driveway or ring the doorbell and ask to see the interior or exterior.

This is one of Richardson's "most successful works and is, perhaps, the best suburban wooden house in America," wrote Henry-Russell Hitchcock in 1936.

Even though the Stoughton House is in busy Cambridge, the style is considered that of a country house. That's why this photograph and diagram are from Arnold Lewis's *American Country Houses of the Gilded Age (Sheldon's "Artistic Country-Seats")*. The photograph is from between 1883, when the house was completed, and 1886–87, when Lewis's book was published. By then, the loggia had been filled. A low wall sits in front of the house.

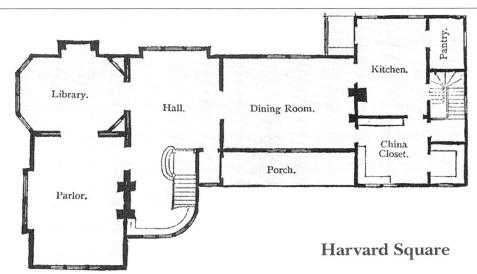

# Green Line

## ROLLING TOUR

**This is not a walking tour of buildings.** It is a rolling tour, on a train, of ghosts of buildings, missing buildings, structures that exist only in photographs, architectural drawings, and memories of a dwindling number of people—structures once dismissed, now missed.

The buildings were designed by H. H. Richardson, "I'll plan anything a man wants, from a cathedral to a chicken coop," he once said. No one ever commissioned him to design a chicken coop, but he did create 12 train stations. Four of them were erected in Newton, Massachusetts, along what is now the Riverside Branch of the Green Line, a light rail commuter line that is part of the Massachusetts Bay Transportation Authority.

This is a tour, from your seat on a Riverside train, of the sites of three Richardson stations, now demolished, two stations built by Richardson's successor architectural firm in his style after he died, and the lone surviving Richardson station in Newton, now neglected and no longer used as a station.

For a biography of Richardson, see page 9.

---

*The tour runs between the Riverside and Chestnut Hill Stations. You can start at either station. (You can also start at any station in between, but that will entail getting on and off one more train, and more waiting for trains to arrive.)*

*It doesn't matter which direction you start in. You'll probably travel in a loop, ending at your starting point. But if you're going to be looking out the window in only one direction, if, say, you're a commuter on the Riverside Branch, you should travel inbound (from Riverside toward Boston). The advantage is that the view is better and the angle less constricted. The disadvantage is that a train on the outbound track could block your view at key moments.*

*(The Riverside Branch is also known as the D Branch—both "D" and "Riverside" appear on Riverside trains—and sometimes as the Highland Branch.)*

Getting to the stations: The stations on this tour, inbound (toward Boston), are Riverside, Woodland, Waban, Eliot, Newton Highlands, Newton Centre, and Chestnut Hill. For directions to the stations, check GPS or mbta.com. The website of the Massachusetts Bay Transportation Authority ("MBTA" for short, or just "the T") will also provide fare information. Commercial bus lines operate service to and from Riverside, which they may simply call "Newton, Massachusetts."

Where to sit: As of this writing, most Riverside trains have two cars of separate designs, one of each design. One has seats perpendicular to the aisle. On an inbound train (toward Boston), sit on the left side, facing forward, but not in the first seat in the front (the window is too small). On an outbound train (away from Boston), sit on the right side, facing forward.

The other car design has seats parallel to the aisle. If you're in this kind of car, you can turn around and look out the window behind you—or switch cars. If you decide to stay, sit on the left side of an inbound train (toward Boston). On an outbound train (away from Boston), sit on the right side.

This tour has three parts—a description of the station sites, and two accompanying essays: one about the influence of Japanese architecture on Richardson's station design, and one about the history and fate of his stations. Read the essays while you're waiting at a station for the train to arrive, while riding on the train, now, or any other time. Read the description of station sites before the train arrives at each station. The sites are listed beginning with Riverside; if you're riding outbound, read the list in reverse order.

An important note about Woodland Station: The Woodland Station that Richardson designed is not the Woodland Station where the MBTA now stops. If you're starting at Riverside, be sure to finish reading about Woodland Station before the train leaves Riverside, and start looking out the window. If you wait until reaching the current Woodland Station to look out the window, you will have missed the one surviving Richardson station on this tour.

If you're traveling toward Riverside, look for Richardson's Woodland Station immediately—and intently—after leaving the current Woodland stop.

**H. H. Richardson: Three Architectural Tours**

In one window is the silhouette of a person. Is the person wearing a station official's hat? Is it the ticket seller? A passenger? At one point, the two prominent windows were turned into an entrance, and filled with a garage door, which is there now. Notice the slight swelling of the ticket window. Photograph courtesy of Houghton Library, Harvard University: Henry Hobson Richardson Photographs of Architectural Projects, 1870–1974, MS Typ 1070 (136).

# Woodland

Richardson designed this station, but died before it was completed in September 1886. It is granite, with a granite chimney and brownstone trim around the windows and doors. It consisted of a waiting room, small baggage room, and two restrooms.

On the trackside were two small inset porches with benches, sort of outdoor waiting rooms. In between them was the ticket window set into a bay window. On the side opposite the tracks is a porte-cochère, a covered carriageway.

Photographs (not included in this book) from the turn of the twentieth century depict the station in a bucolic setting, surrounded by plantings and near a pond. The tracks were not fenced in, as they are now. In 1902, Charles Mulford Robinson wrote that the station's "landscape gardening . . . invites beauty all the year around."

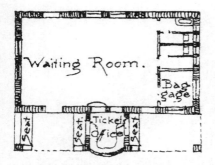

*American Architect and Building News,*
Feb. 26, 1887, reproduced in Jeffrey
Karl Ochsner's *H. H. Richardson:*
*Complete Architectural Works.*

The station may have survived demolition because it was somewhat isolated. It did not serve many passengers, mainly those going to and from Newton Hospital (now Newton-Wellesley Hospital) and the Woodland Park Hotel. (The hotel, no longer standing, was located at the corner of Woodland and Washington Streets.) The station closed even before Boston & Albany trains stopped running past it in 1958.

The station is generally vacant. The Woodland Golf Club stores miscellaneous items and equipment in it, and often leaves it open so that golfers may use the updated restrooms.

The MBTA uses a different location for the current Woodland stop. The Woodland Station designed by Richardson lies between Riverside and the new Woodland stop. While you travel in either direction, it rushes by like an apparition. It is right up against the tracks, so close that it interrupts the fence enclosing the tracks.

The windows and porches are boarded up. The station is on the National Register of Historical Places. This is the only way for the public to view it.

The photograph of Woodland Station on the back cover at the bottom was taken from a passing train in 2013. You can see the garage door that replaced two prominent windows.

The photograph of Woodland Station on the back cover in the middle was taken from the Woodland Golf Course in 2016. A Green Line train rushes by to Boston. Through the station's window, you can see a rolling ladder stored inside.

Newton has two other Richardson buildings: the Bigelow House, which is now condominiums, on Ober Road off Brookline Street in Newton Centre; and the Immanuel Baptist Church, now the Hellenic Gospel Church, at 187 Church Street in Newton Corner.

The man on the right is probably a station official; the man on the left, possibly a constable. On the left, a version of the path up to Beacon Street still exists. Photograph courtesy of Houghton Library, Harvard University: Henry Hobson Richardson Photographs of Architectural Projects, 1870-1974, MS Typ 1070 (134).

## Waban

A "handsome little structure of stone . . . surrounded by a charming park of lawns and shrubbery and ancient forest trees." That's how an 1889 guidebook to Newton described Waban Station. ("Waban" is pronounced to rhyme with "Robin.")

The station, completed in July 1886, three months after Richardson died, was rectangular, with a large overhanging roof supported by brackets. Like the other Richardson stations on this rail line, it was granite with brownstone trim around the windows and doors, with a prominent granite chimney.

If you faced the station with your back to the tracks, the ticket window was in the right front corner, which bulged like the pocket in a pool table. On the side opposite the tracks was a small porte-cochère.

Since the waiting taxis are 1951 or 1952 Plymouths (the cars have taxi signs on top), this photograph dates from sometime between 1951 and 1958, when the station was torn down. The station is grim and grimy. The granite walls can no longer be distinguished from the brownstone trim around the windows. This photograph appeared on Pinterest.com but further information about its source is not available.

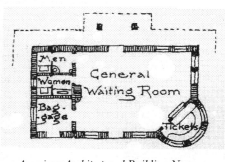

American Architect and Building News, Feb. 26, 1887, reproduced in Jeffrey Karl Ochsner's *H. H. Richardson: Complete Architectural Works*.

Inside, its waiting room was lit by an eyelid dormer in the roof. It had a baggage room, and restrooms for men and women.

In a 1904 article for *House & Garden* magazine, Charles Mulford Robinson wrote that the path leading to Beacon Street created an "effect far lovelier than if the ground between road and station had been cleared for an unnecessary little plaza."

Alas, the ground has been cleared. The park at "little Waban," as Robinson affectionately called it, is gone, and so is the station, which was demolished in 1958. The dell that nestled the station is now a parking lot.

A baggage cart is parked under the Eliot sign. The ticket office is at the far corner. The slate roof, bulges slightly over the ticket window. A bench is tucked past the left roof bracket and under a window to the ticket office. (Richardson created three such benches at Woodland station. See the diagram on page 64.) Photograph courtesy of Houghton Library, Harvard University: Henry Hobson Richardson Photographs of Architectural Projects, 1870-1974, MS Typ 1070 (131).

## Eliot

Eliot Station resembled Woodland Station, except that the ticket window (in a bay window) was on the left, instead of centered. The two ticket windows resembled each other. (See page 63.) The Eliot Station had a porte-cochère on the side opposite the tracks.

The interior consisted of a waiting room, small baggage room, restrooms, and ticket office.

Richardson won the commission for the Eliot, Waban, and Woodland Stations as a package in October 1884, after the Boston & Albany Railroad decided to extend the line from Newton Highlands to Riverside. The neighborhoods were sparsely populated then. One purpose of the stations was to spur the growth of villages around them and create more ridership for the railroad.

*Garden and Forest* magazine wrote in 1889 that before Richardson revolutionized the design of railroad stations, they were "plain, cheap structures," "vulgar little stations," and "wooden boxes which merely displayed the railway company's desire to expend as little money as possible . . . ."

Eliot Station was demolished in 1958, 70 years after its completion, to make room for the current parking lot.

Newton Highlands Station

## Newton Highlands and Newton Centre

Richardson didn't design these stations, but they give you a good idea what his stations on this line looked and felt like: the rugged granite walls, the brownstone trim around the doors and windows, and the prominent roofs supported by heavy wooden brackets. The roofs are hipped, meaning that they slope on all four sides, like the roofs at the Woodland, Waban, and Eliot Stations.

Both Newton Highlands and Newton Centre were designed in Richardsonian style by Shepley, Rutan & Coolidge, an architectural firm that Richardson's top assistants formed after he died. Newton High-

Newton Centre Station

lands was completed in 1887, almost a year after Richardson's death. Newton Centre was completed in 1891.

Both of the stations originally had one level, which is now the upper level on the street. In 1906, the railroad bed was lowered 9 feet, 3 inches so that the tracks wouldn't cross streets and endanger and interfere with automobile traffic. Lower levels were added to both stations. If you look carefully, you'll see that the granite on the lower level is a little darker than the granite on the upper level.

Both stations are or have been occupied by businesses. The interior wainscoting survives in Newton Centre. In Newton Centre, you can still see part of an outlying building, once used for passengers' baggage. As of this writing, it is occupied by a taxi company next to the station.

On the east side of the Newton Highlands station, a path winding through rocks and trees hints at the rustic landscaping that once surrounded some Richardson stations.

**H. H. Richardson: Three Architectural Tours**

Shepley, Rutan & Coolidge designed numerous other stations in Richardson's style after his death. The firm's stations at Riverside, Reservoir, Brookline Hills, and Longwood, all stops on what is now the Riverside Branch of the Green Line, have been demolished. (See page 83.)

The porte-cochère side of Chestnut Hill station. To the right of the tree is the trackside shed, the canopy that protected passengers who were waiting outside. A lantern hangs in the shed. The landscaping that Charles Mulford Robinson described in 1902 (see page 76) is not visible in this photo. It may be outside the camera's range or may have been planted after the photograph was taken. The view is south toward what is now Route 9. The area was rather rural. The photograph is from between 1884, when the station was completed, and 1888, when the photograph was published in Mariana Griswold Van Rensselaer's *Henry Hobson Richardson & His Works.*

## Chestnut Hill

Chestnut Hill was "one of the handsomest little railway stations in the world, a gem of Richardson's architecture," according to an 1889 guidebook to Newton. That same year, *Garden and Forest* called it "perhaps the prettiest and most picturesque of all the great architect's rural stations."

Richardson won the commission for this station after pleasing the Boston & Albany Railroad with his designs for stations in Auburndale (a neighborhood in Newton) and Palmer, Massachusetts.

At the far right, notice the arch that is the porte-cochère's exit. It is the same arch that is in the far left of the first photograph. Above the wooden trackside shed are two windows in the stone gable of the station. Photograph courtesy of Houghton Library, Harvard University: Henry Hobson Richardson Photographs of Architectural Projects, 1870–1974, MS Typ 1070 (126).

Chestnut Hill Station was completed in 1884. The interior held a waiting room, ticket office, and restrooms for men and women. The porte-cochère, the carriage-way, consisted of large Syrian arches so identified with the architect that they are also called Richardsonian arches.

Chestnut Hill was Richardson's only station of this size with a gabled roof (two slopes supported by two gables). The other stations on this line had hipped roofs, which slope on all four sides. The roof swept down from the station, buckling slightly where it met the porte-cochère. The effect was reminiscent of an old New England saltbox house. (Think of a two-story house. If the back eaves

**H. H. Richardson: Three Architectural Tours**

From the outside, the trackside roof seemed architecturally awkward. (See the previous photograph.) From underneath, it seemed to have been an inviting and comfortable space. People, including a station official, lounge in the foreground. Beyond, a person appears to lounge on the stairs. The bulging window between the people is almost certainly the ticket window. Richardson regularly designed curved ticket windows in his train stations. Both hanging lanterns say "Chestnut Hill" in capital letters. Photograph courtesy of Houghton Library, Harvard University: Henry Hobson Richardson Photographs of Architectural Projects, 1870–1974, MS Typ 1070 (130).

are extended down to the first story to create another room in the rear, that's a saltbox.)

Richardson was an eclectic architect, adopting and adapting primarily from Romanesque traditions, a pre-Gothic style from Europe. This station represented one of the few examples of his borrowing from New England architecture.

The trackside of the station was less successful. The roof covering the broad stairs was ungraceful. And the dormer was un-Richardsonian: triangular with a grid of small windows. One would have expected to see an eyelid dormer, as at Waban, or at least an arched dormer, similar to what Richardson's successors designed at Newton Centre.

Tearing down the station and paving its grounds was a double transgression, for it destroyed the artistry of two masters: H. H. Richardson and Frederick Law Olmsted, the pioneering landscape architect who designed Boston's series of parks called the Emerald Necklace and co-designed New York's Central Park.

This is how Charles Mulford Robinson rhapsodized in *House & Garden* in 1902 about Olmsted's creation at Chestnut Hill: "There is a park-like approach, roads and paths winding luxuriously down to the little station building, where a stunning stone arch throws its protecting cover from wind and rain over the carriage drive. The street is not visible from the railroad, and the little park is graded gradually to the low level of the station. Two noble old willows adorn a stretch of lawn, and the shrubbery here has been planted with unusual skill and artistic excellence. One can imagine a business man choosing Chestnut Hill for his place of residence for no other reason than the soothing charm with which its little station would daily wait his return and the lingering caress of beauty with which it would send him forth."

A parking lot now covers the park. The station's demise came so ignominiously that its date doesn't seem to be recorded. It was torn down around 1960.

# The Japanese Influence on Richardson's Stations

**One of Richardson's hallmarks** was eclecticism. Among the architectures and styles that he borrowed from or paid tribute to were Romanesque, Syrian, Queen Anne Revival, Colonial—and Japanese.

After two centuries of isolation, Japan allowed contact with the West in the mid-nineteenth century. The reopening of Japan sparked Japanese influence on Western aesthetics, an influence called Japonism in English, *Japonisme* in French.

A major figure in educating Bostonians about Japanese life, culture, and aesthetics was Edward S. Morse, a biologist who went to Japan in 1877 to research coastal brachiopods. In 1882, he delivered 12 lectures in Boston, whose newspapers widely reported on them. Richardson cannot be placed at one or more of Morse's lectures, and Morse's photographs and drawings of Japanese buildings have not been located among Richardson's extensive collection of images of

buildings that he drew on for inspiration. Although many Bostonians became familiar with Morse's depictions of Japanese architecture, it is unknown if Richardson was among them.

Richardson's embrace of Japanese forms is obvious in some works. Dragons are carved into beams in Austin Hall at Harvard Law School (see pages 47-50) and on his railroad station in North Easton, Massachusetts. The Japanese influence was subtler in other works. Architect Scott Tulay pointed out in his senior college thesis that the lines of some Richardson train stations resemble some rural Japanese houses, inns, and temples that stood in the nineteenth century.

A line drawing of Richardson's Woodland Station is "startlingly like" a line drawing that Morse did of a country inn in

Top: The roof line of Waban Station resembled farmers' houses in Japan. (So did Woodland and Eliot Stations.) Middle: View of a farm village, Japan from the E. S. Morse Collection. Bottom: "Harvesting Rice," View of Japan from the E. S. Morse Collection.

Rikuzen, Japan, wrote Margaret Henderson Floyd. She was a Richardson scholar and Tulay's academic advisor. The roofs of the stations in Newton were not simply hipped; they were Japanese hipped roofs in the rural tradition. Richardson's stations in Newton were "the first coherent group of Japanese-influenced architectural designs in America," she wrote.

RAILROAD STATION, WOODLAND.

Top: Eldon Deane drew Woodland Station for the 1888 book *Henry Hobson Richardson & His Works* by Marianna Griswold Van Rensselaer. Middle: E. S. Morse drew "Country Inn, Rizuken, Japan." It appeared in his 1885 book *Japanese Homes and Their Surroundings*. The country inn and Woodland Station resemble each other. Bottom: The inn's gable resembles the trackside gable of Chestnut Hill Station.

# The History and Fate of Richardson's Stations

**H. H. Richardson was the right man** at the right time and place. In the 1880s, the Boston and Albany (B&A) Railroad began to beautify its stations. One reason was that Massachusetts state law limited the railroad's profit to a 10 percent return. By building distinguished stations and landscaping them attractively, the B&A invested excess profits—and also expanded the total investment base on which its 10 percent return was calculated.

Also in the 1880s, the B&A acquired, improved, and lengthened track beds to create the Newton Circuit Railroad, a commuter train loop between Boston and Newton. The circuit ran from Boston to Riverside on what is now the Riverside Branch of the MBTA's Green Line. At Riverside, trains headed back to Boston on a route near the commuter train tracks that now run alongside the Massachusetts Turnpike.

A vice president of the B&A Railroad was James Rumrill, Richardson's friend and classmate from Harvard. Both had belonged to the Hasty Pudding Club, the Porcellian Club, and Pieran Sodality, an orchestra.

A director of the B&A was Charles Sprague Sargent, who graduated from Harvard three years after Richardson and had also belonged to the Hasty Pudding Club. Sargent was also a director of the Arnold Arboretum and later editor of *Garden and Forest* magazine. He was a man devoted to trees, landscaping, and aesthetics. Sargent's estate in Brookline was across the street from Richardson's home and studio, and the two men were friends.

So it made sense that Richardson received the commission in April 1883 to build a station at Chestnut Hill. In October 1884, the B&A awarded Richardson commissions to build three additional stations, along new trackage, at Eliot, Waban, and Woodland. The Circuit Railroad officially began service in May 1886.

*Garden and Forest* wrote that Richardson "showed for the first time what such a building ought to be." What a railroad station should be was a gateway to the suburbs—which in Boston then were rather rural.

Mariana Griswold Van Rensselaer, Richardson's friend and biographer, wrote that he "strove first of all clearly to express the building's purpose—to mark the fact that a station is not a house, but a shelter, not a place to live but to wait under. The roof is the chief feature not the walls. These are always low and the plan as compact as possible, while the roof is massive and broad."

Any commuter who has waited out of the rain or snow under the broad roofs of the stations at Newton Centre or Newton Highlands— stations designed in the Richardsonian style, but not by Richardson— can attest that these are indeed commuter-friendly roofs.

Jeffrey Karl Ochsner, a scholar of Richardson, wrote, "Beneath this roof traffic flow was kept as simple as possible, from sheltering porte-cochère, through the waiting rooms, past the ticket booth, to the

**H. H. Richardson: Three Architectural Tours**

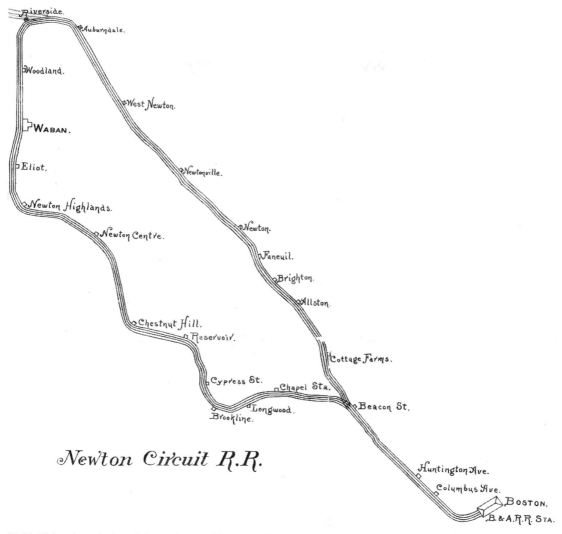

*Newton Circuit R.R.*

H. H. Richardson designed the stations at Chestnut Hill, Eliot, Waban, Woodland, Auburndale, and Brighton. (The Green Line tour includes the first four stations.) His successor firm, Shepley, Rutan & Coolidge, designed the stations at Longwood, Brookline Hills (designated on the map as "Cypress St."), Reservoir, Newton Centre, Newton Highlands, Riverside, and Allston. Stations at Newton Centre, Newton Highlands, Woodland, and Allston survive. Francis R. Kowsky, an architectural historian, wrote that "the landscape and stations along the Newton Circuit...had the character of a linear park...." From Plan of Lands, Waban Station – Newton, belonging to Charles D. Page and Fred H. Henshaw, Newton, Mass. 1889, Albert F. Noyes, Surveyor. Courtesy of Historic Newton.

broad trackside shed. Passage from train to carriage or carriage to train was sheltered at every step."

The Boston & Albany Railroad ended commuter service on what is now the Riverside Branch on May 31, 1958. The Massachusetts Bay

Transportation Authority (then known as the Metropolitan Transit Authority) started service on July 4, 1959. One of the authority's first acts was to tear down Richardson's stations along the Riverside Branch to accommodate more parked automobiles.

Richardson's stations at Chestnut Hill, Eliot, and Waban have been destroyed. Woodland station is no longer a station or even a stop. Richardson's stations in Auburndale (a neighborhood of Newton) and Brighton (a neighborhood of Boston) were destroyed when the Massachusetts Turnpike was built.

Elsewhere, Richardson's stations survive in Framingham and Wellesley, Massachusetts. In Wellesley, most of the street side of the facade has been mutilated. The rest of the exterior survives, but the interior has been stripped. Both are near stops on the rail system, but not used inside as stations. They are or have been occupied by businesses.

Richardson's stations in Holyoke, Palmer, and North Easton, Massachusetts, are not used as rail stations or stops. Of the 12 railroad stations that Richardson designed, only the Union Passenger Station in New London, Connecticut, is still used for its original purpose. The New London station escaped a few demolition deadlines in the 1970s before it was finally saved and renovated.

In 1914, J. H. Phillips wrote of Richardson's railroad stations in the *Architectural Record*: Their "substantial walls of local stone gave an air of permanence and stability."

For most of his stations on what is now the Green Line, it was only an air.

# Appendix

## HAYDEN BUILDING AND STONY BROOK GATEHOUSE

## In addition to the four surviving Richardson buildings

in the Copley Square area, Boston (not the Greater Boston area, but Boston itself) has two more: the Hayden Building and the Stony Brook Gatehouse.

# Hayden Building
**681—683 Washington Street, also called 8 La Grange Street,
south corner of Washington and La Grange Streets**

*Getting there by public transportation: The Hayden Building is within walking distance of Boylston Station on the Green Line, Chinatown Station on the Orange Line, and the Chinatown Stop on the Silver Line 4 and 5.*

*If you're getting off the Orange Line inbound, leave the station and turn left. You're on Washington Street. At the next intersection, the Hayden Building is kitty-corner.*

*If you're getting off the Orange Line outbound, leave the station and turn right. You're on Washington Street. At the next intersection, the Hayden Building is across La Grange Street.*

The Hayden Building in 1977, the year it was rediscovered to be Richardson's work. On the La Grange Street side (the long side), the entrance to what is now the residences (to the right of the empty billboard and behind the street sign) was filled with cinder blocks, leaving a small doorway. Photograph by Bob Stanton for the Boston Landmarks Commission.

*If you're getting off the Green Line, either inbound or outbound, leave the station and continue in the direction that the exit points you. You're walking parallel to Tremont Street. At the corner, which is the intersection of Boylston and Tremont Streets, cross kitty-corner. Walk on Tremont Street. Take your first left onto La Grange Street. The Hayden Building is on the right, at the end of the block, on the corner.*

The Hayden Building is not as elaborate and awe-inspiring as Trinity Church, but it is significant, is admirable in its understated utilitarian way, and is Richardson's work and therefore worth viewing. Its compactness makes it easier to comprehend than, say, Trinity Church.

The main facade is the narrow one on Washington Street. On the second story, three windows are grouped under one low arch. The lintels (above the windows) are saw-toothed, which is visible in the photograph. The saw-tooth pattern carries around the corner onto one window on the La Grange Street facade. On the third and fourth stories on Washington Street, the three windows are each under a separate arch—but Richardson used the same arch extending between the two stories to unify them. The fifth floor has four simpler rectangular windows arranged over the three arches below. The cornice, consisting of brackets under the eaves, is solid stone, although broken in places.

The decoration is at the fourth-story level. Most of it is at the building's right corner. The carved foliage at the corner is repeated on top of the pilasters (flattened columns). Less elaborate carved foliage continues on the La Grange Street facade at the same level.

Richardson designed fewer than ten commercial buildings. Four of them were in Boston and this is the only one left here. Completed in 1876, the Hayden Building is significant because it foreshadowed the Marshall Field Wholesale Store, a Richardson masterpiece that occupied a half-block in Chicago and was completed in 1887. As famous as Trinity Church is, the Marshall Field store "is probably the most famous of Richardson's buildings," wrote Jeffrey Karl Ochsner. Photographs of it "appear in virtually every history of modern architec-

**H. H. Richardson: Three Architectural Tours**

ture," he added. A photograph of it appears on the cover of a book by one Richardson scholar. Richardson talked about the Marshall Field store on his deathbed. (See page 35-36.)

The Marshall Field Wholesale Store, Chicago. Public domain photograph.

Because the Marshall Field store provided many design solutions for Chicago skyscrapers in the last two decades of the nineteenth century, the Hayden Building was a forerunner of the skyscraper, the Boston Landmarks Commission has written. The Marshall Field Wholesale Store was demolished in 1930, but we do have the Hayden Building, a smaller reminder of it.

The Hayden Building is like an Old Master's painting that is found at a yard sale. It wasn't until 1977, 101 years after it was completed, that the building was recognized as Richardson's work. It took so long because Richardson designed the building for his wife's family (her maiden name was Hayden), he didn't charge for the design, and the building wasn't entered into his firm's records. When the records were used to catalog Richardson's works, the Hayden Building was left out. Cynthia Zaitevksy, an architectural historian, finally discovered or rediscovered the Hayden Building as Richardson's.

The building, which the National Register of Historic Places listed in 1980, almost didn't survive demolition plans, redevelopment schemes, and a fire. It fell on hard times when its neighborhood was the Combat Zone, Boston's red light district, which is practically gone as of this writing—but its few remnants are next to the building on La Grange Street. When the building was renovated in the

2010s, reels of abandoned pornographic movies were found inside. The renovation returned the ground floor to retail space. Each of the four upper floors became a residence.

The retail facade is not original. An early photograph (not in this book) shows that the entry was a portico inset into the building, with a column at the corner of Washington and La Grange Streets. The only original aspect of the first-story facade is at the left edge: a pilaster topped with a capital. The capital is of some sort of foliage. Above the foliage is saw-toothed carving, echoing the second-story windows. The entry on La Grange Street to the residences was not cut into the facade during the renovation; Richardson probably designed the entry there.

The Hayden Building is largely made of Longmeadow brownstone. Its lintels and arches are granite.

# Stony Brook Gatehouse
## 125 The Fenway

*Getting there by public transportation: Take the Heath Street Branch/E Branch of the Green Line to the Northeastern University stop. If you're traveling outbound (away from downtown), get off the train and turn left; if you're traveling inbound (toward downtown), get off the train and turn right. Turn right again at the next intersection, Forsyth Street. Forsyth Street ends in a T at Hemenway Street. Continue across the street on a walkway as if Forsyth Street continued. Cross the Fenway (a street) and the building is right in front of you.*

*If you're taking the Orange Line, get off at Ruggles Station. Walk on Forsyth Street. Cross Huntington Avenue and follow the directions above, starting with "Forsyth Street ends in a T . . . ."*

Visiting the Stony Brook Gatehouse is for zealous Richardson aficionados, such as those who want to see all of his extant work. (That includes the author.) To be frank, making a trip solely to visit it might not be worth it. Visit it if you're nearby, such as at the Museum of Fine Arts or in the Fens.

The gatehouse was completed in 1882 to regulate the flow of water from Stony Brook into the Muddy River. It contained floodgates; hence, the building's name as a gatehouse. Its original location was a stone's throw upstream (to the left) and closer to the river. It was moved in 1905. No longer needed as a gatehouse, it was restored in 2010 as the Shattuck Visitor Center for the Emerald Necklace Conservancy.

The gatehouse is the product of one of many collaborations between two luminaries, architect H. H. Richardson and landscape architect Frederick Law Olmsted. Olmsted designed the Emerald Necklace, Boston's series of parks that includes the Fens. (They also collaborated on Chestnut Hill Station. See page 76.)

In 1910, a nearly identical gatehouse was built next to it. Some decline to attribute it to Richardson. However, after an architect's death, if someone replicates his or her work, right down to the shape of the brackets under the eaves, it is more than fair to call it the architect's design. The 1910 gatehouse still houses pumping equipment and is used to control water flow.

In the 1882 gatehouse, the modern office space—a surprising amount—is of course not original. The front door, with its strap hinges, is probably original. The building is listed on the National Register of Historic Places.

Both gatehouses are constructed with Roxbury puddingstone. The stone is rust-colored, except where it is gray at the lower levels.

# Bibliography

*Around the Station: The Town and the Train.* Framingham, Mass.: Danforth Museum, 1978.

Campbell, Robert. "A Robert A. M. Stern Building Embodies Tradition at Harvard Law: Law School Building Is a Bit Pompous." *Boston Globe* 11 Dec. 2011.

Fleming, Malcolm M. "The Saving of Henry Hobson Richardson's Union Station, New London, Connecticut." *American Art Review* Volume 2 July–August 1975: 29-39.

Floyd, Margaret Henderson. *Henry Hobson Richardson: A Genius for Architecture.* New York: Monacelli Press, 1997.

*Guidebook to Harvard University: Celebrating Crimson Key Society's 50th Year.* Cambridge: Crimson Key Society, 1998.

"The Hayden Building: Boston Landmarks Commission Study Report." Boston Landmarks Commission, 1977.

"Henry Hobson Richardson." *Harvard Monthly,* Oct. 1886.

Hitchcock, Henry-Russell. *The Architecture of H. H. Richardson and His Times.* Cambridge: MIT Press, 1981.

Lewis, Arnold. *American Country Houses of the Gilded Age (Sheldon's "Artistic Country-Seats").* New York: Dover Publications, 1982 (originally published 1886–87).

Lyndon, Donlyn. *The City Observed: Boston: A Guide to the Architecture of the Hub.* New York: Vintage Books, 1982.

Morse, Edward S. *Japanese Homes and Their Surroundings.* New York: Dover Publications, 1961 (originally published 1885).

Ochsner, Jeffrey Karl. *H. H. Richardson: Complete Architectural Works.* Cambridge: MIT Press, 1988.

Ochsner, Jeffrey Karl. "Architecture for the Boston & Albany Railroad: 1881–1894." *Journal of the Society of Architectural Historians* Volume XLVII June 1988: 109–31.

O'Gorman, James F. *H. H. Richardson: Architectural Forms for an American Society.* Chicago and London: University of Chicago Press, 1987.

O'Gorman, James F. *Living Architecture: A Biography of H. H. Richardson.* New York: Simon & Schuster, 1997.

Phillips, J. H. "The Evolution of the Suburban Station." *Architectural Record* Volume 36 Aug. 1914: 122–27.

"The Railroad-station at Chestnut Hill." *Garden and Forest* Volume 2 3 April 1889: 159–60.

Robinson, Charles Mulford. "A Railroad Beautiful." *House & Garden* Volume 2 Nov. 1902: 564–70.

Robinson, Charles Mulford. "Suburban Station Grounds." *House & Garden* Volume 4 April 1904: 182–87.

Southworth, Susan and Michael. *The Boston Society of Architects' A. I. A. Guide to Boston.* Chester, Conn.: Globe Pequot Press, 1984.

Stern, Robert A. M. and Graham, Wyatt S. *Designs for Learning: College and University Buildings by Robert A. M. Stern Architects.* New York: Monacelli Press, 2016.

Sweetser, M. F. *King's Handbook of Newton, Massachusetts.* Boston: Moses King Corporation, 1889.

Tulay, Scott. "Edward S. Morse and Japanese Architecture: Inspiration for H. H. Richardson in the 1880s." Medford, Mass.: Tufts University (senior honors thesis), 1992.

Van Rensselaer, Mariana Griswold. *Henry Hobson Richardson & His Works*. New York: Dover Publications, 1969 (originally published 1888).

Wilson, Susan. *Boston Sites and Insights: A Multicultural Guide to Fifty Historic Landmarks in and Around Boston*. Boston: Beacon Press, 1994.

backbayhouses.org

historicboston.org

# Acknowledgments

Deborah Fogel; Judah Levine; Jeffrey Karl Ochsner;
Michael Platt, Woodland Golf Club;
Emerald Necklace Conservancy; Joel Leeman, Esq.;
Mary Haegert, Houghton Library, Harvard University;
Cambridge Historical Society;
Angelo Van Bogart, Editor, Old Cars Weekly;
Rev. John R. Odams and Earl Norman, First Baptist Church of Boston;
Sara L. Goldberg, Historic Newton; the Boston Athenaeum;
Crimson Key Society; Bruce Wood, KMW Architecture;
Peter Morris Dixon, Robert A. M. Stern Architects; Paul Rocheleau;
Rob Roche, Shepley Bulfinch;
Doreen Hann, who's more than a book designer

And thank you to Peter Acosta, the driver of the ice cream truck, with the American flag flying, that was parked on the plaza in front of Trinity Church when I showed up, yet another time, trying to get a photograph for the cover of this book. After he and I chatted about why I was there, he kindly moved his truck temporarily—to a place he told me he was not supposed to be. When I tried to buy a lemon ice, he insisted that it was on the house.

**Ken Bresler is a writer and native of Newton, Massachusetts.** He is the author of *The Witch Trial Trail and the Harvard Witch Walk: The People and Places of Boston and Harvard Connected with the Salem Witch Trials* (1992); and *Poetry Made Visible: Boston Sites for Poetry Lovers, Art Lovers & Lovers* (2017).

Bresler graduated from Harvard Law School and attended classes in Austin Hall. His passion for Richardson's work predates his entering law school.

Of the 45 surviving buildings that *H. H. Richardson: Complete Architectural Works* credits to Richardson, Bresler has seen 40, as of this writing.

Made in the USA
Columbia, SC
08 September 2018